Note to Parents and Teachers

The READING ABOUT: STARTERS series introduces key science vocabulary to young children while encouraging them to discover and understand the world around them. The series works as a set of graded readers in three levels.

LEVEL 1: BEGINNING TO READ follows guidelines set out in the National Curriculum for Year 1 in schools. These books can be read alone or as part of guided or group reading. Each book has three sections:

• Information pages that introduce new words. These key words appear in bold throughout the book for easy recognition.
• A lively story that recalls this vocabulary and encourages children to use these words when they talk and write.
• A quiz and picture index ask children to look back and recall what they have read.

IS IT ALIVE? looks at LIVING THINGS. Below are some answers and activities related to the questions on the information spreads that parents, carers and teachers can use to discuss and develop further ideas and concepts:

p. 7 *What things are alive but do not move much?* Plants are alive but move very slowly – many flowers close their petals at night and open wide in the morning. Some animals move slowly and may stay still for a long time, such as snails and limpets.

p. 9 *What other ways do animals move?* Encourage children to widen vocabulary using words like scuttle, slither, crawl or hop. You could ask them to act out the movements.

p. 11 *What do you need to be strong and healthy?* As well as good food and plenty of water, our bodies need fresh air, exercise, rest and a good night's sleep.

p. 13 *What can you see, hear, smell and feel in a garden?* Encourage children to explore with their senses in a park or garden. They can see and hear insects and birds, smell the flowers, or feel the rough trunk of a tree or a soft clump of grass or moss.

p. 15 *How can you tell that you are growing?* As we grow we get taller and heavier – that's why we grow out of our clothes and shoes. Our nails and hair grow too.

p. 17 *What does a plant need to live and grow?* As well as nutrients from the soil (food) and water, plants need lots of sunlight to help them grow.

p. 21 *Why does a truck need a driver?* A driver starts and stops the engine and steers the truck (so it does not bump into things). A truck can't do these things by itself.

p. 23 *Seashells were once alive. Where can you find them?* You find shells on the beach. They once grew on the backs of animals such as clams, limpets and mussels.

ADVISORY TEAM

Educational Consultant
Andrea Bright – Science Co-ordinator, Trafalgar Junior School, Twickenham

Literacy Consultant
Jackie Holderness – former Principal Lecturer in Primary Education, Westminster Institute, Oxford Brookes University

Series Consultants
Anne Fussell – Early Years Teacher and University Tutor, Westminster Institute, Oxford Brookes University

David Fussell – C.Chem., FRSC

CONTENTS

© Aladdin Books Ltd 2006

Designed and produced by
Aladdin Books Ltd
2/3 Fitzroy Mews
London W1T 6DF

First published in
Great Britain in 2006 by
Franklin Watts
96 Leonard Street
London EC2A 4XD

A catalogue record for this book is available from the British Library.

ISBN 0 7496 6291 3

Printed in Malaysia

All rights reserved

Editor: Jim Pipe

Design: Flick, Book Design and Graphics

Thanks to:
• The pupils of Trafalgar Infants School, Twickenham for appearing as models in this book and to Armen, Zara and Mia Babasyan and Aran Vartanyan for appearing as models in the story.
• Debbie Staynes for helping to organise the photoshoots.
• The pupils and teachers of Trafalgar Junior School, Twickenham and St. Nicholas C.E. Infant School, Wallingford, for testing the sample books.

Photocredits:
l-left, r-right, b-bottom, t-top, c-centre, m-middle
Front cover tl, tm & tr, 5t, 10br, 23t, 31tr, 32br — Photodisc. Front cover b, 2bl, 7t, 8, 22bl, 31ml, 32mlt — Marc Arundale/Select Pictures. 2tl, 6t, 18, 19t — TongRo. 2ml, 11l, 15tr, 16, 32mrt, 32mr — USDA. 3, 15b, 31mr — US Fish & Wildlife Service. 4, 13tr, 14, 32tr — Digital Vision. 5br, 17tr, 24tl & mr, 25mr, 26 both, 27mr & bl, 28br, 29bl, 30, 32mlb — Jim Pipe. 6br, 12, 22tr, 24bl &br, 27t, 28tl, 29tr, 32ml, 32tr — Comstock. 7br, 8tl, 11r, 17b, 19br, 20, 32mrb — Corbis. 8m — Stockbyte. 8br, 10m — John Foxx Images. 13b — Corel. 21, 31bl, 32bl — Scania. 25bl — Ingram Publishing.

Starters

LIVING THINGS

Is It Alive?

by Sally Hewitt

Aladdin/Watts

London • Sydney

You are **alive**.

You move about.

You eat and drink.

You see and taste and feel.

You are an **animal** called a human.
Animals are **alive**.

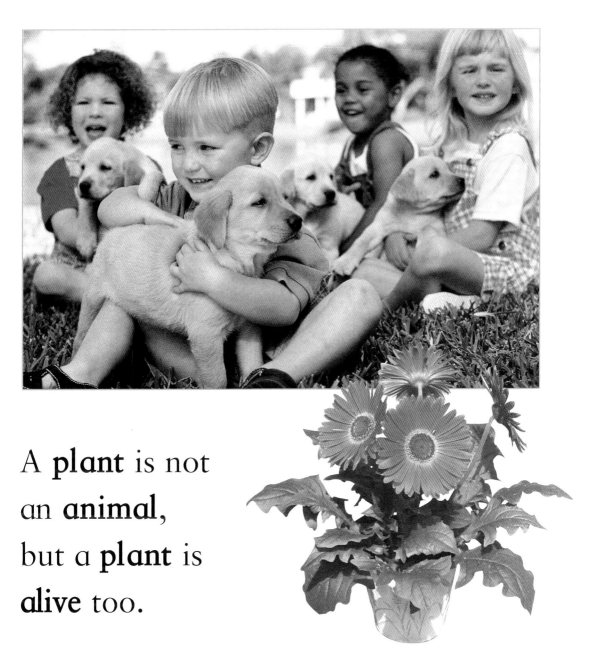

A **plant** is not
an **animal**,
but a **plant** is
alive too.

• What plants and animals can you think of?

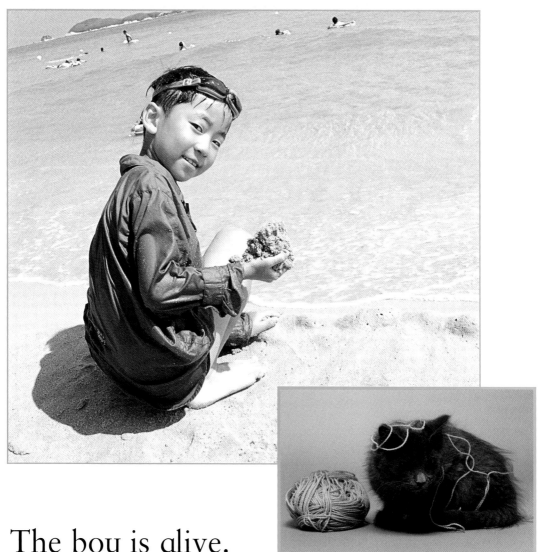

The boy is alive.
But sand is **not alive**.

The kitten is alive too.
But a ball of string is **not alive**.

These things are **not alive**.

A toy mouse can't move unless you pull the string.

A ball doesn't move until you kick it.

• What things are alive but do not move much?

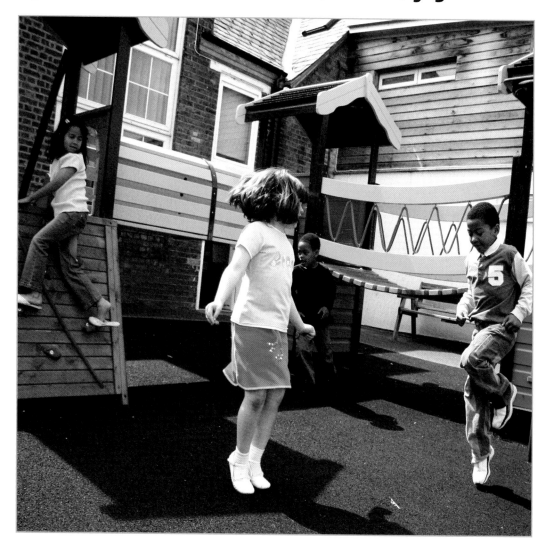

Things that are alive can **move**.

People can **walk**, run and jump.
How else can you **move**?

Animals **move** in all kinds of ways.

Fish **swim**.

Birds **fly**.

How does a snail **move**?

• What other ways do animals move?

An animal needs **food** and **water**.
So do plants.

You need **food** and **water**.
They give you **energy** to
move and grow.

A goat eats leaves and branches.
A lion hunts for meat to eat.

 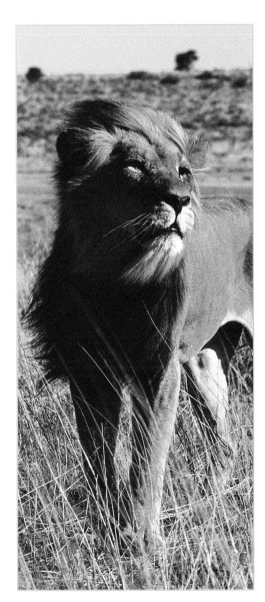

• What do you need to be strong and healthy?

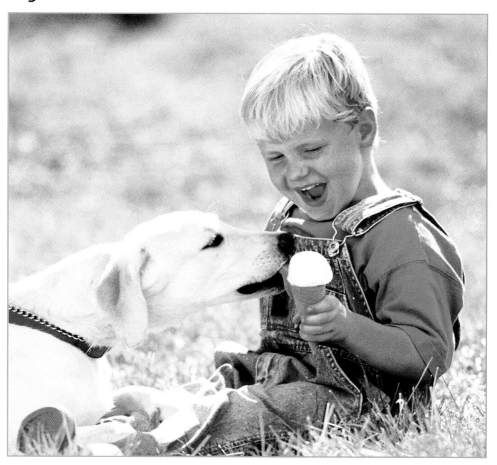

Things that are alive can **sense**
the world around them.

You can see the dog.
You can feel its soft fur.
What can the dog smell and taste?

A frog has big eyes
to see all around.

A wild cat's
big ears hear
small sounds.

• What can you see, hear, smell and feel in a garden?

Things that are alive **grow**.

Animals have **young**.
Young grow up to look
like their parents.

You **grow** into an adult.

A piglet **grows** into a pig.

A chick **grows** into a bird.

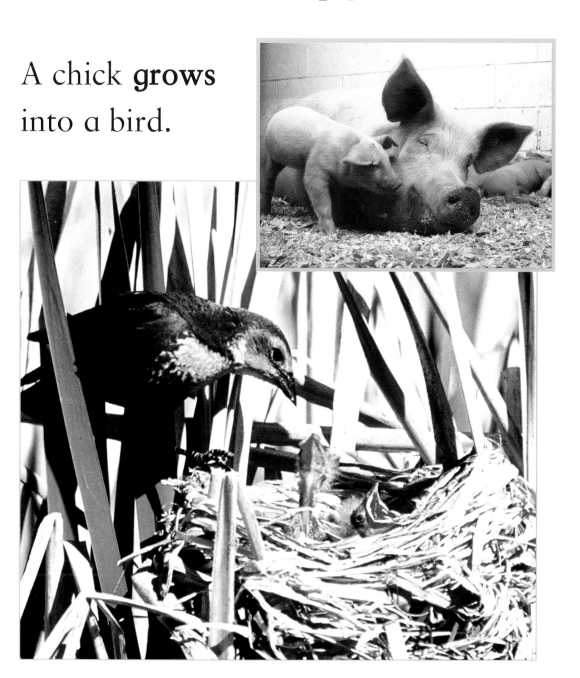

• How can you tell that you are growing?

My new word: **seed**

Plants are alive. They take food and water from the soil.

Plants can't walk, swim or fly but they do move.

Sunflowers turn their heads to the Sun.

A **seed** grows into a plant.

A little acorn is a **seed**.
It grows into
a big oak tree.

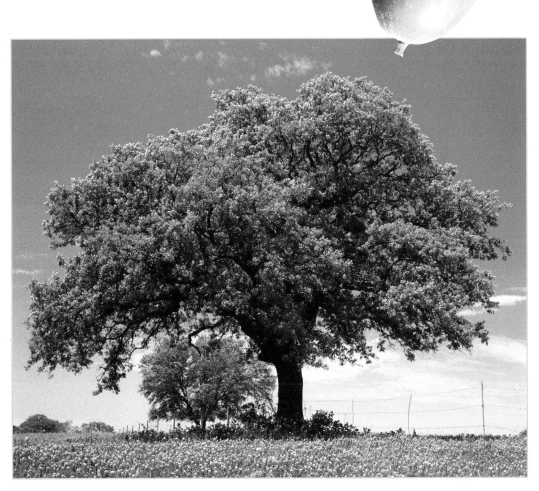

• What does a plant need to live and grow?

Look at this picture. What is alive?

People play in the water.
Fish swim in the **sea**. They are alive.

The **sea** moves up and down the
beach, but the **sea** is not alive.

18

Trees move in the wind.
Trees are plants, so they are alive.

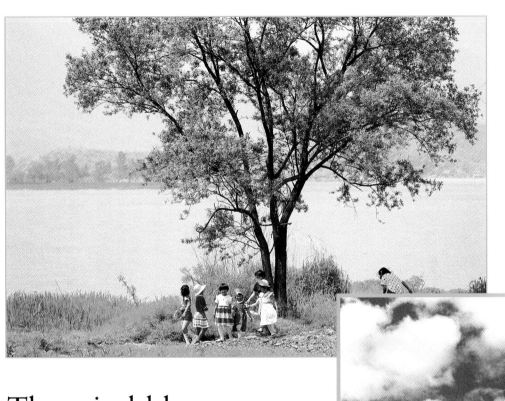

The wind blows
clouds across the sky.

But **clouds** are
not alive.

• What other living things are in the sea?

19

Machines can move and make things.

But **machines** do not eat like us. They do not grow.

Machines are not alive.

A big truck is a **machine**.
An **engine** helps it move fast.

But a truck can't move by itself.
It needs a driver.

• Why does a truck need a driver?

This bat is made of wood.
Wood comes from a tree.

The wood was **once alive**,
but the bat is
not alive!

A woolly scarf
was **once alive**.

Wool is hair cut
from a sheep.

This fossil was **once alive**.

It is an animal that was alive millions of years ago.

We know about dinosaurs from fossils.

• Seashells were once alive. Where can you find them?

LOOKING AFTER TEDDY

Look out for words about **living things**

My friend Millie and her family are on holiday. Dad, Joss and I **walk** over to their house.

We have to feed the cat Smokey and the goldfish Flash, and **water** the **plants**.

Our dog Bluey wants to come too!

"Millie has left Teddy behind!" I say.
"Let's look after Teddy," says Joss.
"He can keep Leo
the lion company!"

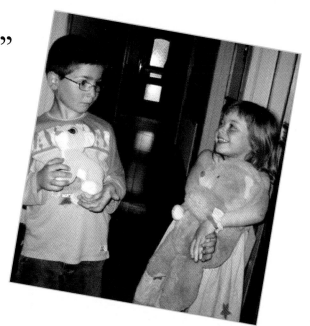

"We'll look after
the **animals** and
plants first,"
says Dad.

"Why?" I ask.

"Because they are
alive. Teddy is **not**
alive. Nor is Leo."

"How do you know Teddy and Leo are **not alive**?" I ask.
I give Teddy a cuddle.

"Teddy and Leo
don't eat and drink,"
says Dad.

"We do!" we say.
"That's because you
are **alive**," laughs Dad.

"Smokey needs to eat
and drink," says Dad.

"Just like Bluey," I say.

Dad gives Smokey **food** to eat and milk to drink.

Joss gives Flash some **food**. Flash **swims** up and eats it.

We **water** the **plants**.

Joss looks out of the window. He says, "It's raining!"

"That will **water** the **plants** outside," says Dad. "They need a drink."

"Look," says Dad. "Smokey is **moving** in that bag. He can **sense** something."

"I can **move**, and so can Teddy!" I say. "So can Leo!" says Joss.

We make the toys **fly**.

"But toys can't **move** all by themselves," says Dad.

Smokey sits in the window. He watches the **clouds** and **trees**.

"If I look after Teddy, will he **grow** big and strong like me?" I ask.

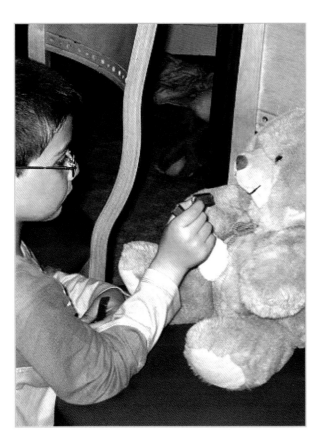

"No," says Dad. "Teddy won't **grow**."

"But Milly will be pleased you are looking after him."

"And Milly's mum will be pleased we are looking after Smokey, Flash and the **plants**," says Jess.

"And I'm pleased I'm looking after you!" says Dad.

Things that are **alive** like you can:

- **Move**
- **Feel**
- **Eat and drink**
- **Grow**

Snail

Draw pictures of things that are **alive**. Check that they do all these things.

QUIZ

Are you a **plant** or an **animal?**

Answer on page 5

Is a toy mouse **alive?**

Answer on page 7

What will a chick **grow** into?

Answer on page 15

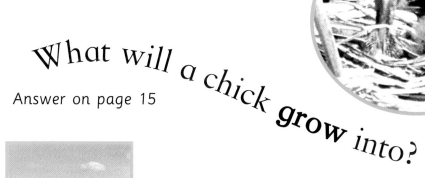

How do you know
a **machine** is not **alive?**

Answer on page 20-21

Did you know the answers? Give yourself a

Do you remember these words about **living things**?
Well done! Can you remember any more?

 alive
page 4

not alive
page 6

 move
page 8

food
page 11

 sense
page 12

grow
page 15

 seed
page 17

cloud
page 19

 machine
page 21

once alive
page 23